HOMEMADE SALAD DRESSINGS

50 SIMPLE, DELICIOUS AND HEALTHY *DIY SALAD DRESSING RECIPES*

LOW CARB, GLUTEN FREE

Published by The Fruitful Mind

www.fruitfulbooks.com

Disclaimer

Table of Contents

SPECIALTY BLENDER DRESSINGS (NUTRIBULLET, MAGIC BULLET, ETC.) 109

Introduction

There are few things that sound healthier than a fresh salad, robust with crisp, flavorful vegetables and fruits. The perfect salad has textures and flavors combining together just right, leaving you satisfied and nourished. Just stop for a moment and picture it in your mind. Imagine dark, crisp greens that lay the foundation for colorful, fresh from the garden vegetables, each bite a perfect union of freshness. Or maybe what you crave and desire is a luscious fruit salad, with just the perfect hint of sweetness combined with fresh greens of savory nuts and cheeses.

Salads offer virtually endless options for healthy meals and snacks. With a little imagination and a willingness to explore new ingredients, salads can be endlessly satisfying and anything but boring and mundane. The salad, which was once the classic sign of a low calorie dieter, has become so much more than it was in the past. Salads today are flavorful and hearty, and can be created to accommodate any dietary lifestyle from low carbohydrate, low sodium, reduced calorie and more modern dietary trends such as Paleo.

There is one element of a salad that really brings it to life that can take any one salad and give it several different personalities. That element is of course, the salad dressing. Dressings can be savory or sweet, a tangy vinaigrette or lusciously creamy. We each have our favorites and feel that a salad just isn't complete without it. Unfortunately, many of the dressings that we use are loaded with bad fats and hidden sugars, laying the road to sabotage for even the most conscientious consumer. This is especially true if you venture out of your home into your favorite eatery to enjoy a salad. Common ingredients included hydrogenated oils, sugar and an abundance of salt.

The common salad dressing can take a light four hundred calorie salad and turn it into an eight hundred calorie disaster, and that isn't even mentioning the damage that is being done with trans fats and sodium. We consume these salads often times thinking the dressing is harmless, after all how bad can just that little bit of dressing be? The unfortunate truth is that the dressing can be very bad, and that combined with the fact that many of us overindulge with salad dressings means that our best attempts at being healthy become anything but. The best plan of action is to ditch the dressing, at least the unhealthy ones you have been using, and embrace the delicious world of simple and healthy homemade dressings. There are numerous advantages to creating your own dressings, among them are:

•You pick the ingredients. What do you really know about the ingredients that are used in your favorite commercially produced dressing? Do you even recognize all of the ingredients on the label? When you make your own dressings, you are creating a whole, clean food with ingredients that you choose, at their peak of freshness and quality.

•You pick the flavor. When you make your own dressing, you can create any flavor profile that you desire and tailor it specifically to your individual tastes. Maybe you like a little bit more tanginess or prefer something that just lingers in the background to accentuate the natural flavor of the salad, without altering the real flavor of the original elements. The choice is up to you, and it can even be different every time, depending on what you want, not what some company decides will best appeal to the masses.

•You can adjust any dressing recipe to accommodate your unique dietary considerations. Whatever your dietary goals are, if you are striving to lose unwanted pounds, lower your blood pressure or follow a particular dietary lifestyle such as low carbohydrate or vegan, you can adjust any of the recipes in this book, or ones that you create yourself to fit into your dietary needs.

•You can mix it up. Have you ever purchased a jar of dressing because it sounded good and then only used a couple of portions out of it, leaving the rest to sit in the refrigerator, expiring before it was used because your craving was satisfied (or unsatisfied), and you just didn't desire it anymore? There have been times when my own refrigerator has been a condiment graveyard. This is no longer a concern when you make your own dressings. You can make only the amount that you want, leaving you free to explore a new taste or recipe next time.

•Homemade dressings are economical. Serving per serving, homemade dressings cost a fraction of what commercially prepared dressings do, especially when you consider the quality of ingredients involved. Making your own dressings allows you a higher quality and more nutrition for a lower price.

•Making your own dressing barely takes any more time than you would spend pondering the different options in your grocery store. In no more than five minutes you can create your own fresh and healthy dressings.

•Finally, making your own dressings is enjoyable. You can let your imagination and creativity guide the way and turn your favorite classics into incredible new tastes. Just a few simple changes to a single recipe can completely change the flavor profile. Dressings are inexpensive to make and when made in smaller batches, require little commitment. This means that you are free to explore, guilt free. Have fun with your dressings and recreate your favorite salads with the addition of new flavors.

The Making of a Healthy Salad Dressing

What exactly is it about these healthy homemade salad dressings that make them superior in taste and healthy qualities than dressings that you may find on your grocer's shelves? When these recipes were crafted there were several key standards of quality that were kept in mind. These qualities include:

Quality whole ingredients: Almost every recipe included in this book is based on whole, natural ingredients. The exceptions to this are the addition of minor ingredients such as light mayonnaise or sugar free preserves that are added in small amounts to enhance flavor and texture in some recipes. Otherwise, you will find each recipe based upon heart healthy oils, a variety of naturally flavored vinegars, thick and creamy Greek yogurt and buttermilk, all with additional natural ingredients to create and enhance flavor.

The healthiest choices of ingredients: Vinaigrettes are made with oils that are rich in omega 3 fatty acids such as extra virgin olive oil and walnut oil. When lower fat options provide a better health benefit without reducing flavor, they have been chosen in favor of their higher fat substitutes. Examples of this include low fat sour cream or low fat mayonnaise. Fresh ingredients are chosen over canned or processed ingredients every time.

Natural sweeteners are included over artificial ones: Honey and brown sugar are used rather than artificial sweeteners such as aspartame. Of course, if for dietary reasons you find it better for your own health to choose a sugar substitute, than by all means follow the dietary guidelines set by your physician or nutritional counselor.

Serving size is taken into consideration: You will notice that even though many of the recipes yield a similar amount of dressing, the amount of servings will vary among them. This is for several reasons. First of all, each type of dressing will adhere differently to your salad. Vinaigrettes are thinner, meaning that they lightly coat a larger amount of salad than a thicker, cream based dressing. Vinaigrettes also pack more flavor per bite. This means that less vinaigrette is needed per serving, which is also important because the proportion of oil can sometimes leave vinaigrettes a little higher in calorie content, something that is important for those who are on calorie conscious dietary plans. Processed salad dressings rarely take these factors into consideration and when they do, the solution is usually to compensate with unhealthy, processed ingredients.

The recipes in this book are created to meet a larger range of dietary needs and goals; however, you will notice that there are three healthy eating categories that are specifically mentioned. Those are Gluten Free, Low Carb and Vegan. Each recipe is noted with which of these dietary lifestyles it fits within the guidelines of.

Most dressings in this book are gluten free, however as many of us know, gluten is hidden in sneaky places and that has been taken into consideration with the recipes that have not been listed as gluten free. Those recipes may contain ingredients such as miso, soy sauce or even pickles which sometimes contain gluten due to the spices included. Each of those recipes can be made gluten free with a deletion or knowledgeable substitution of ingredients.

Vegan recipes contain no animal products, which also includes honey. If you are a vegan who eats honey than you will find that an even larger portion of the recipes in this book will suit your needs without substitution.

Low carbohydrate recipes are those that include 2 grams or less of net carbohydrates per serving.

As you begin to look over the delicious salad dressing recipes presented to you in this book, you will notice that they are created to appeal to a wide variety of healthy goals. Not every recipe in this book will appeal to each and every person or dietary lifestyle. However, each recipe can be amended slightly to accommodate any taste or need. For example, you may come across a vinaigrette that looks tasty, but is a little higher in calorie content than you would prefer due to the base of olive, or other heart healthy, oil.

To make this more low calorie friendly, you simply reduce the amount of oil and replace it with vinegar, citrus juice or even something like buttermilk which will maintain some of the vinaigrette qualities while significantly reducing calories. Additionally, if you are striving for a low carbohydrate option but can't get your mind off of a fruit based dressing, try substituting part of the fruit and honey (or other sweetener) with a smaller amount of sugar free fruit preserves, which pack major fruit flavor into smaller servings. If you desire a vegan dressing, simply change out ingredients for vegan substitutes, such as rice or soy milk instead of buttermilk or another sweetener rather than honey.

About the Ingredients

You will notice that through the fifty dressings there are key ingredients that are used throughout. This is because these ingredients are healthy, tried and true. If you keep these staple ingredients in your pantry and refrigerator, you can have a healthy homemade dressing any time.

EXTRA VIRGIN OLIVE OIL: Rich in Omega 3 Fatty Acids, olive oil makes for a rich, heart healthy base to vinaigrettes and an emulsifying addition to some creamier dressings. While dressings that contain larger amounts of olive oil will be higher in calories, this oil offers other advantages for your health that outweigh the calorie content unless you follow a calorie restrictive eating plan.

CANOLA OIL: A nice alternative to olive oil when the nutty taste of olive oil doesn't suit or is too overpowering for certain dressings.

BUTTERMILK: Naturally low in fat, buttermilk is a wonderful tangy base when you desire a creamier base to your dressings.

VINEGARS: Many dressings contain at least some vinegar. Vinegar gives your dressing tanginess, bite and balance. There is an incredible variety of vinegars to choose from including white wine vinegar, red wine vinegar, balsamic vinegar, apple cider vinegar, rice vinegar, raspberry vinegar, sherry vinegar, champagne vinegar and more. Try changing out the varieties of vinegar in your dressing to create new tastes.

HERBS: The right herb can make a dressing. In most cases, fresh herbs have been used rather than dry; although you can substitute dry herbs if you have limited access to fresh herbs. Just make sure that you use lesser of the dried variety than what is called for with the fresh herbs. When using fresh herbs, choose them carefully for quality and wash and trim them as appropriate before using.

Salt: Most recipes have an addition of salt for no other reason than flavor enhancement. The amount of salt used per recipe can be altered to suit your dietary needs if you are on a limited or low sodium diet.

LOW FAT SOUR CREAM AND LOW FAT MAYONNAISE: These lighter versions

of their full fat counterparts offer flavor and texture without the calorie and fat content that can be detrimental to your diet. If you are on a low carbohydrate diet, or one that favors full fat versions of these products then just change them out in amounts equal to those given in the recipe.

HONEY: In most cases if a recipe calls for some

sort of sweetener, honey has been chosen. Honey blends well with the oils, vinegar and dairy ingredients of many of the recipes. It is all natural and comes in several different varieties, each lending its own characteristic flavor. If you choose not to use honey, you may substitute it with any other sweetener in amounts suited towards your own taste preference.

Now you know that making your own healthy salad dressings is simple and requires just a few basic ingredients. Read on and enjoy discovering new dressing options that you will come to treasure for years in the future.

THE CLASSICS

This class of dressings contains all of the ones that have won our hearts for years and sometimes even generations. The only difference is that these variations take not only your health into consideration, but also your desire to enjoy fresh and wholesome ingredients. Enjoy these delicious dressing staples with guilt free indulgence.

Garlic Italian Dressing

Low Carb, Gluten Free

Yields: 1½ cup dressing, approximately 16 servings

Ingredients:

1 cup extra virgin olive oil

¼ cup champagne vinegar

1½ tablespoons red wine vinegar

1 teaspoon honey

2 garlic cloves, crushed and finely minced

2 tablespoons pimento or jarred roasted red peppers, finely chopped

1 tablespoon red onion, finely chopped

1 teaspoon crushed rosemary

1 teaspoon dried basil

½ teaspoon dried oregano

½ teaspoon salt

1 teaspoon coarse ground black pepper

Directions:

Combine the champagne vinegar and red wine vinegar in a bowl. Whisk to blend.

Slowly add in the olive oil, blending with a whisk the entire time until the oil and vinegars are blended.

Whisk in the honey thoroughly before adding the garlic, pimento or roasted red peppers and onion.

Season with rosemary, basil, oregano, salt and black pepper. Mix well. Use immediately or store in an airtight jar. Shake well before use.

Nutritional Information: Calories 96, Fat 10g, Protein 0g, Net Carbohydrates 1g

Basic Balsamic Vinaigrette

Gluten Free, Low Carb, Vegan

Yields: 1½ cup dressing, approximately 16 servings

Ingredients:

1 cup extra virgin olive oil

¼ cup balsamic vinegar

1 teaspoon brown sugar

1 tablespoon shallots, diced

½ teaspoon salt

½ teaspoon black pepper

Directions:

Combine the balsamic vinegar and brown sugar in a bowl. Mix until the brown sugar is dissolved.

Slowly add in the extra virgin olive oil, whisking the entire time until well blended.

Add in the shallots and stir to mix. Season with salt and black pepper.

Use immediately, or store in an airtight jar in the refrigerator. Shake well before using.

Nutritional Information: Calories 91, Fat 10g, Protein 0g, Net Carbohydrates 1 g

Perfect Honey Mustard Dressing

Gluten Free

Yields: 1½ cup dressing, approximately 16 servings

Ingredients:

1 cup canola oil

2 tablespoon champagne vinegar

¼ cup Dijon mustard

3 tablespoons honey

1 teaspoon dried thyme

⅛ teaspoon cayenne powder

½ teaspoon salt

1 teaspoon coarse ground black pepper

Directions:

Combine the Dijon mustard and honey in a bowl. Whisk until well blended.

Add in the champagne vinegar and whisk until fully incorporated.

Slowly add the canola oil, whisking the entire time until the dressing is blended and lightly emulsified.

Season with thyme, cayenne, salt and black pepper.

Serve immediately or store in the refrigerator in an airtight container. Shake well before using.

Nutritional Information: Calories 106, Fat 10g, Protein 0g, Net Carbohydrates 3g

Tangy Yogurt Based Thousand Island Dressing

Low Carb

Yields: 1½ cup dressing, approximately 12 servings

Ingredients:

½ cup plain Greek yogurt

2 tablespoons light mayonnaise

¼ cup sweet chili garlic sauce

2 tablespoons shallots, diced

2 tablespoons sweet pickle, diced

1 egg, hardboiled and chopped

1 teaspoon paprika

½ teaspoon salt

½ teaspoon black pepper

Directions:

Combine the plain Greek yogurt and light mayonnaise in a bowl.

Mix in the sweet chili garlic sauce, shallots, sweet pickle and egg.

Season with the paprika, salt and black pepper.
Mix well.

Serve immediately or store in the refrigerator in
an airtight jar.

Nutritional Information: Calories 24, Fat 1g,
Protein 2g, Net Carbohydrates 2g

Lightened Up Ranch

Low Carb, Gluten Free

Yields: 1¾ cup dressing, approximately 14 servings

Ingredients:

1 cup low fat buttermilk

½ cup plain Greek yogurt

1 teaspoon rice vinegar

2 cloves garlic, crushed and finely minced

¼ cup fresh parsley, chopped

1 tablespoon fresh chives, chopped

1 tablespoon fresh dill, chopped

1 teaspoon paprika

½ teaspoon salt

1 teaspoon coarse ground black pepper

Directions:

Combine the buttermilk and Greek yogurt. Whisk until well blended and smooth.

Whisk in the rice vinegar until well blended.

Season with garlic, parsley, chives, dill, paprika, salt and black pepper. Stir to mix.

Serve immediately or store in the refrigerator in an airtight container. Shake well before use.

Nutritional Information: Calories 14, Fat 0g, Protein 2g, Net Carbohydrates 1g

Creamy Blue Cheese Dressing

Low Carb

Yields: Makes 1 cup dressing, approximately 8 servings

Ingredients:

¼ cup low fat buttermilk

¼ cup plain Greek yogurt

1 ½ tablespoon lemon juice

2 tablespoons light mayonnaise

¾ cup blue cheese, crumbled

1 tablespoon shallots, sliced

1 teaspoon Worcestershire sauce

½ teaspoon salt

1 teaspoon white pepper

Directions:

Place the blue cheese in a bowl along with the light mayonnaise and mash until creamy, but with some small chunks of blue cheese remaining.

In another bowl combine the buttermilk, lemon juice and Greek yogurt. Whisk until creamy.

Blend the buttermilk mixture with the blue cheese mixture. Mix well.

Add the shallots and Worcestershire sauce and then season with salt and white pepper. Mix well. Serve immediately or store in the refrigerator in an airtight jar until ready to serve.

Nutritional Information: Calories 54, Fat 4g, Protein 2g, Net Carbohydrates 2g

Unforgettable Simple Vinaigrette

Low Carb, Gluten Free

Yields: 1½ cup dressing, approximately 16 servings

Ingredients:

1 cup extra virgin olive oil

¼ cup red wine vinegar

1 tablespoon stone ground mustard

1 teaspoon honey

½ teaspoon salt

1 teaspoon coarse ground black pepper

Directions:

In a bowl combine the red wine vinegar, stone ground mustard and honey. Whisk until blended.

Slowly add in the olive oil, whisking constantly until the dressing is blended and lightly emulsified.

Season with salt and black pepper. Serve immediately or store in an airtight container in the refrigerator. Shake well before use.

Nutritional Information: Calories 96, Fat 10g, Protein 0g, Net Carbohydrate 1g

Eggless Caesar Dressing

Low Carb, Gluten Free

Yields: 1½ cups dressing, approximately 12 servings.

Ingredients:

1 cup plain Greek yogurt

3 tablespoons extra virgin olive oil

¼ cup fresh lemon juice

3 cloves garlic, crushed and minced

6 anchovies, chopped

¼ cup fresh grated parmesan cheese

2 teaspoons coarse ground black pepper

Directions:

Place the garlic, anchovies, parmesan cheese, olive oil and lemon juice in a blender.

Blend until a smooth, thin paste forms.

Add in the Greek yogurt and black pepper. Blend until well mixed. Serve immediately or store in the refrigerator in an airtight container. Shake well before using.

Nutritional Information: Calories 60, Fat 5g, Protein 3g, Net Carbohydrates 1g

Greenest Goddess Dressing

Low Carb, Gluten Free

Yields: 1½ cup dressing, approximately 12 servings.

Ingredients:

½ cup Greek yogurt

½ cup low fat sour cream

2 tablespoons lemon juice

1 tablespoon chives, chopped

½ cup fresh parsley, chopped

¼ cup fresh tarragon, chopped

2 tablespoon fresh dill, chopped

½ teaspoon salt

1 teaspoon white pepper

Directions:

In a bowl combine the Greek yogurt, low fat sour cream and lemon juice. Whisk well until blended. If you like a thinner dressing, add a little extra lemon juice or water.

Place the yogurt mixture in a blender along with the chives, parsley, tarragon, dill, salt and white pepper. Blend until smooth.

Serve immediately or store in the refrigerator in an airtight jar.

Nutritional Information: Calories 20, Fat 1g, Protein 4g, Net Carbohydrates 1g

Honey Lemon Poppy Seed Dressing

Gluten Free, Low Carb

Yields: 1½ cup dressing, approximately 16 servings.

Ingredients:

1 cup extra virgin olive oil

¼ cup apple cider vinegar

1 tablespoon lemon juice

2 tablespoons honey

1 tablespoon honey mustard or Dijon mustard (depending on taste preference)

1 tablespoon toasted poppy seeds

½ teaspoon salt

Directions:

Combine the apple cider vinegar, lemon juice, honey and mustard in a bowl. Whisk until well blended.

Stir in the poppy seeds and season with salt.

Slowly add in the olive oil, whisking constantly until blended and slightly emulsified. Serve immediately or store in the refrigerator in an airtight jar.

Nutritional Information: Calories 99, Fat 10g, Protein 0g, Net Carbohydrates 2g

NEW FAVORITES: VINAIGRETTES

There is something about the perfect vinaigrette with just the right amount of vinegar and spices that leave your mouth watering and wanting just a little more. Vinaigrettes are perfect for dressing a variety of salads because they lightly coat the ingredients, without being heavy or overpowering. For this reason you will notice that the amount of servings per cup or cup and a half of vinaigrette is a little less than a creamy dressing. This is to accommodate the lighter and "clingier" nature of the vinaigrette. Many, although not all, of the vinaigrettes in this section are crafted with the traditional ratio of 1 cup oil to ¼ cup vinegar. If you like a tangier (or lower calorie) version, simply reduce the amount of oil and increase the amount of vinegar to your liking.

Champagne and Shallot Vinaigrette

Low Carb, Gluten Free, Vegan

Yields: 1½ cup dressing, approximately 16 servings

Ingredients

1 cup extra virgin olive oil

¼ cup champagne vinegar

2 teaspoons lemon juice

2 tablespoons shallots, minced

2 teaspoons fresh rosemary, chopped

1 teaspoon salt

½ teaspoon black pepper

Directions:

Place the champagne vinegar and lemon juice in a bowl and mix together.

Slowly add in the olive oil, whisking constantly until all of the oil is blended in.

Stir in the shallots, rosemary, salt and black pepper.

Serve immediately or store in the refrigerator in an airtight jar. Shake well before using.

Nutritional Information: Calories 90, Fat 10g, Protein 0g, Net Carbohydrates 0g

Asiago Garlic Vinaigrette

Low Carb, Gluten Free

Yields: 1½ cup dressing, approximately 16 servings

Ingredients

1 cup extra virgin olive oil

¼ cup balsamic vinegar

1 head roasted garlic

1 tablespoon fresh oregano

½ teaspoon salt

1 teaspoon coarse ground black pepper

½ cup asiago cheese, grated

Directions:

Place the roasted garlic cloves, balsamic vinegar, oregano, black pepper and asiago cheese in a blender. Blend briefly to puree the garlic and mix the ingredients.

Slowly pour in the olive oil, blending as it is added, until the oil is entirely incorporated and the dressing is lightly emulsified.

Serve immediately or store in the refrigerator in an airtight jar. Shake well before using.

Nutritional Information: Calories 100, Fat 11g, Protein 1g, Net Carbohydrates 1 g

Greek Style Vinaigrette

Low Carb, Gluten Free

Yields: 2 cup dressing, approximately 16 servings

Ingredients:

1 cup extra virgin olive oil

¼ cup rice vinegar

2 teaspoons lemon juice

½ cup feta cheese, crumbled

¼ cup roasted red bell peppers, minced

1 tablespoon kalamata olives, finely minced

2 cloves garlic, crushed and finely minced

2 tablespoons fresh parsley, chopped

1 tablespoon fresh oregano, chopped

Directions:

Combine the rice vinegar and lemon juice in a bowl and mix.

Slowly add in the olive oil, whisking the entire time until the oil is completely incorporated.

Place the feta cheese in a bowl and mash as much as possible before pouring the vinaigrette on top. Whisk the vinaigrette and feta cheese together.

Add in the roasted red bell peppers, kalamata olives, garlic, parsley and oregano. Whisk or mix until well blended.

Serve immediately or store in the refrigerator in an airtight container. Shake well before using.

Nutritional Information: Calories 102, Fat 11g, Protein 1g, Net Carbohydrates 1g

Walnut Herb Vinaigrette

Low Carb, Vegan

Yields: 1½ cups dressing, approximately 16 servings

Ingredients:

¾ cup extra virgin olive oil

¼ cup walnut oil

¼ cup apple cider vinegar

2 cloves garlic, crushed and finely minced

½ cup fresh basil, chopped

½ cup fresh parsley, chopped

½ cup walnuts, chopped

½ teaspoon salt

1 teaspoon black pepper

Directions:

Place all of the ingredients in a blender and blend until combined and lightly emulsified.

Serve immediately or store in the refrigerator in an airtight jar. Shake well before using.

Nutritional Information: Calories 144, Fat 16g, Protein 1g, Net Carbohydrates 1g

Sweet and Spicy Pecan Vinaigrette

Low Carb, Gluten Free
Yields: 1½ cup dressing, approximately 16 servings

Ingredients:

¾ cup canola oil
¼ cup walnut oil
¼ cup apple cider vinegar
2 tablespoons spicy mustard
1 tablespoon honey
½ cup pecans, chopped
1 tablespoon fresh rosemary, chopped
½ teaspoon salt
1 teaspoon black pepper
Pinch cayenne powder

Directions:

Combine the apple cider vinegar, spicy mustard, honey, pecans, rosemary, salt, black pepper and cayenne in a blender. Blend until smooth.

Slowly add first the canola oil and then the walnut oil, blending until completely combined and slightly emulsified.

Serve immediately or store in the refrigerator in an airtight jar. Shake well before use.

Nutritional Information: Calories 151, Fat 16g, Protein 1g, Net Carbohydrates 2g

Spicy Ginger Vinaigrette

Low Carb, Vegan

Yields: 1½ cup, approximately 16 servings

Ingredients:

1 cup canola oil

1 teaspoon sesame oil

¼ cup lime juice

2 tablespoons miso paste

2 cloves garlic, crushed and minced

2 teaspoons crushed red pepper flakes

2 tablespoon fresh grated ginger

½ teaspoon salt

Directions:

Combine the sesame oil, lime juice, miso paste, garlic, crushed red pepper flakes, ginger and salt in a blender. Blend briefly to mix.

Slowly add in the canola oil while blending until the oil is fully incorporated and the dressing is lightly emulsified.

Serve immediately or store in the refrigerator in an airtight jar. Shake well before using.

Nutritional Information: Calories 127, Fat 14g, Protein 0g, Net Carbohydrates 1g

Roasted Red Pepper Vinaigrette

Low Carb, Gluten Free, Vegan

Yields: 1½ cup dressing, approximately 16 servings

Ingredients:

1 cup extra virgin olive oil

¼ cup sherry vinegar

1 tablespoon lemon juice

½ cup roasted red peppers

2 cloves garlic, crushed and minced

1 tablespoon fresh tarragon

1 teaspoon salt

1 teaspoon black pepper

Directions:

Combine the sherry vinegar, lemon juice, roasted red pepper, garlic, tarragon, salt and black pepper. Blend well.

Slowly add in the olive oil, blending until the oil is fully mixed in.

Serve immediately or store in the refrigerator in an airtight container. Shake well before using.

Nutritional Information: Calories 91, Fat 10g, Protein 0g, Net Carbohydrates 1g

Cranberry Gorgonzola Vinaigrette

Low Carb, Gluten Free

Yields: 2 cups dressing, approximately 16 servings

Ingredients:

1 cup extra virgin olive oil

¼ cup sherry vinegar

½ cup gorgonzola cheese, crumbled

¼ cup dried cranberries

1 tablespoon shallots, diced

2 teaspoons fresh rosemary, chopped

½ teaspoon salt

1 teaspoon coarse ground black pepper

Directions:

Place the sherry vinegar, gorgonzola cheese, dried cranberries, shallots, rosemary, salt and black pepper in a blender. Blend until mixed a paste has formed.

Slowly add in the olive oil while blending until the oil is fully blended in. Serve immediately or store in the refrigerator in an airtight jar. Shake well before serving.

Nutritional Information: Calories 110, Fat 11g, Protein 1g, Net Carbohydrates 2g

Cipollini Bacon Vinaigrette

Low Carb, Gluten Free

Yields: 2 cups dressing, approximately 20 servings

Ingredients:

½ cup extra virgin olive oil plus one tablespoon

½ cup balsamic vinegar

¼ cup bacon, cooked and crumbled

½ cup Cipollini onion

1 tablespoon fresh thyme

2 teaspoons fresh oregano

½ teaspoon salt

1 teaspoon coarse ground black pepper

¼ cup fresh grated parmesan cheese

Directions:

Heat one tablespoon of the olive oil in a skillet over medium heat. Add the Cipollini onion and cook until caramelized, approximately 3-4 minutes. Remove from heat.

Place the balsamic vinegar in a bowl and slowly add in the olive oil. Whisk constantly until the oil is completely mixed in.

Stir in the bacon, caramelized onion, thyme, oregano, salt, black pepper and parmesan cheese. Stir or whisk until well blended.

Serve immediately or store in the refrigerator in an airtight jar. Shake well before using.

Nutritional Information: Calories 165, Fat 17g, Protein 1g, Net Carbohydrates 1g

Spicy Orange Vinaigrette

Low Carb, Gluten Free, Vegan

Yields:1½ cup dressing, approximately 12 servings

Ingredients:

½ cup extra virgin olive oil

½ cup sherry vinegar

2 tablespoons orange juice

1 tablespoon shallots, diced

1 serrano pepper, diced

1 tablespoon fresh cilantro, chopped

Directions:

Combine the sherry vinegar and orange juice in a bowl.

Slowly add in the olive oil, whisking constantly until the oil is blended in.

Add the shallots, Serrano pepper and cilantro. Mix well. Serve immediately or store in the refrigerator in an airtight jar. Shake well before using.

Nutritional Information: Calories 82, Fat 9g, Protein 0g, Net Carbohydrates 1g

NEW FAVORITES: RICH AND CREAMY

Do you love the rich and decadent creaminess of a dressing but tend to avoid them because of the high fat and calorie content? If that is the case, then this section is for you. These dressings are made with high protein, low fat options such as Greek yogurt and low fat buttermilk. The results are dressings that meet your needs for creaminess and exceed your expectations in taste and flavor.

Horseradish Dill Dressing

Low Carb, Gluten Free

Yields: 1½ cup dressing, approximately 12 servings

Ingredients:

½ cup low fat buttermilk

½ cup low fat sour cream

¼ cup prepared horseradish

¼ cup fresh dill, chopped

¼ cup fresh parsley, chopped

½ teaspoon salt

1 teaspoon coarse ground black pepper

Directions:

In a bowl whisk together the buttermilk and sour cream. Blend until smooth.

Add in the horseradish, dill, parsley, salt and black pepper. Mix until well blended.

Serve immediately or store in the refrigerator in an airtight jar. Shake well before using.

Nutritional Information: Calories 21, Fat 2g, Protein 1g, Net Carbohydrates 2g

Dijon Caper Dressing

Low Carb, Gluten Free

Yields: 1½ cup dressing, approximately 12 servings

Ingredients:

½ cup plain Greek yogurt

¼ cup low fat mayonnaise

¼ cup Dijon mustard

¼ cup white wine vinegar

¼ cup capers, chopped

2 cloves garlic, crushed and minced

2 tablespoons fresh chives, chopped

½ teaspoon salt

1 teaspoon black pepper

Directions:

In a bowl combine the Greek yogurt, mayonnaise, Dijon mustard and white wine vinegar. Mix well.

Add in the capers, garlic, chives, salt and black pepper. Mix well. If you prefer a thinner dressing, add a little lemon juice until the desired consistency is reached.

Serve immediately, or store in the refrigerator in an airtight jar until ready to use.

Nutritional Information: Calories 19, Fat 1g, Protein 1g, Net Carbohydrates 1g

Ginger Curry Dressing

Low Carb, Gluten Free

Yields: 1½ cup dressing, approximately 12 servings

Ingredients:

½ cup plain Greek yogurt

½ cup low fat mayonnaise

¼ cup lemon juice

1 tablespoon curry powder

2 teaspoons fresh grated ginger

1 tablespoon honey

Directions:

Combine the Greek yogurt, mayonnaise and lemon juice. Whisk until well blended.

Stir in the lemon juice, curry powder, ginger and honey. Mix until all of the ingredients are well combined.

Serve immediately or store in the refrigerator in an airtight jar until ready to use.

Nutritional Information: Calories 30, Fat 2g, Protein 1g, Net Carbohydrates 1g

Creamy Parmesan Dressing

Low Carb, Gluten Free

Yields: 1½ cup dressing, approximately 12 servings

Ingredients:

1 cup plain Greek yogurt

¼ cup low fat buttermilk

2 tablespoon red wine vinegar

4 cloves garlic

¼ cup fresh grated parmesan cheese

½ teaspoon salt

1 teaspoon coarse ground black pepper

Directions:

Place the garlic, parmesan cheese, salt and black pepper in a blender. Blend until a paste forms.

Combine the Greek yogurt, low fat buttermilk and red wine vinegar in a bowl. Mix well using a whisk. You may adjust the amount of buttermilk used to accommodate your preference in the thickness of the dressing.

Add the garlic paste from the blender into the yogurt mixture. Mix well until completely blended.

Serve immediately or store in the refrigerator until ready to serve.

Nutritional Information: Calories 20, Fat 1g, Protein 3g, Net Carbohydrates 1g

Avocado Bacon Dressing

Low Carb, Gluten Free

Yields: 2 cups dressing, approximately 16 servings

Ingredients:

1 cup plain Greek yogurt

1 avocado, cubed

2 tablespoons extra virgin olive oil

2 tablespoons rice milk or low fat buttermilk

2 cloves garlic

¼ cup bacon, cooked and crumbled

1 tablespoon fresh chives, minced

1 tablespoon fresh dill, chopped

Directions:

Add the olive oil, rice milk, garlic, bacon, chives and dill to a blender. Blend until a paste forms.

Add in the yogurt and avocado to the blender and blend until smooth.

Serve immediately or store in the refrigerator in an airtight jar until ready to serve.

Nutritional Information: Calories 64, Fat 5g, Protein 4g, Net Carbohydrates 2g

Creamy Cucumber Herb Dressing

Low Carb, Gluten Free

Yields: 1½ cup dressing, approximately 12 servings

Ingredients:

1 cup cucumber, peeled and sliced

2 cloves garlic

¼ cup extra virgin olive oil

¼ cup plain Greek yogurt

1 tablespoons lemon juice

¼ cup fresh dill, chopped

¼ cup fresh basil, chopped

1 teaspoon salt

1 teaspoon black pepper

Directions:

Place the cucumber and garlic in a blender. Blend until smooth.

Add in the olive oil, Greek yogurt and lemon juice. Blend until creamy and emulsified.

Pour the dressing into a bowl and season with dill, basil, salt and black pepper. Mix well.

Serve immediately or store in the refrigerator in an airtight jar until ready to serve.

Nutritional Information: Calories 44, Fat 4g, Protein 1g, Net Carbohydrate 1g

Creamy Chimichurri Dressing

Low Carb, Gluten Free

Yields: 1½ cup dressing, approximately 12 servings

Ingredients:

1 cup plain Greek yogurt

¼ cup extra virgin olive oil

¼ cup red wine vinegar

3 cloves garlic

¼ cup fresh parsley, chopped

¼ cup fresh cilantro, chopped

1 tablespoon fresh oregano

1 teaspoon fresh thyme

½ teaspoon salt

Directions:

Place the garlic, parsley, cilantro, oregano, thyme and salt in a blender. Blend until a paste forms.

Add in the yogurt, olive oil and red wine vinegar. Blend until creamy and emulsified.

Serve immediately or store in the refrigerator until ready to serve.

Nutritional Information: Calories 53, Fat 4g, Protein 2g, Net Carbohydrates 1g

Pine Nut Dressing

Low Carb, Gluten Free

Yields: 1½ cup dressing, approximately 16 servings

Ingredients:

½ cup plain Greek yogurt

½ cup extra virgin olive oil

¼ cup red wine vinegar

2 cloves garlic

¼ cup pine nuts

1 teaspoon lemon zest

1 tablespoon fresh basil, chopped

Directions:

Place the garlic, pine nuts, orange zest and basil in a blender. Blend until pulverized.

Add in the Greek yogurt, olive oil and vinegar. Blend until creamy.

Serve immediately or store in the refrigerator until ready to serve.

Nutritional Information: Calories 75, Fat 8g, Protein 1g, Net Carbohydrates 1g

ON THE SWEET SIDE: FRUIT BASED DRESSINGS

Fruit based dressings have become increasingly popular in recent years. Fruit adds a complexity to dressing that is both a little sweet, a little sour and often times pairs surprisingly well with herbs and other savory elements. Some of these fruit dressings offer the perfect counterbalance to salads that contain rich ingredients such as nuts and cheeses, while others are perfect to accentuate the brightness of refreshing salads with light fruit elements. This collection of fruit based dressings is perfect for exploring and discovering new favorites.

Honey Lemon Dressing

Gluten Free. Low Carb

Yields: 1½ cup dressing, approximately 16 servings

Ingredients:

½ cup extra virgin olive oil

½ cup walnut oil

½ cup lemon juice

1 tablespoon honey

¼ cup walnuts, finely chopped

Directions:

Combine the lemon juice and honey in a bowl.

Slowly add in the olive oil and walnut oil, whisking constantly until the oils are well incorporated.

Add in the walnuts and stir well.

Serve immediately, or store in an airtight jar in the refrigerator. Shake well before using.

Nutritional Information: Calories 138, Fat 15g, Protein 1g, Net Carbohydrates 2g

Raspberry Vinaigrette

Gluten Free, Low Carb

Yields: 1½ cup dressing, approximately 12 servings

Ingredients:

½ cup canola oil

¼ cup raspberry vinegar

1 cup fresh raspberries

2 teaspoons honey

¼ cup golden raisins

1 tablespoon fresh tarragon, chopped

Directions:

Place the raspberry vinegar, fresh raspberries, honey, raisins and tarragon in a blender.
Blend until a puree forms.

Slowly add in the canola oil while blending until the oil is fully mixed in.

Serve immediately or store in the refrigerator in an airtight container until ready to use.

Nutritional Information: Calories 75, Fat 7g, Protein 0g, Net Carbohydrates 2g

Sweet Grapefruit Vinaigrette

Gluten Free, Low Carb

Yields: 1½ cup dressing, approximately 16 servings

Ingredients:

1 cup canola oil

¼ cup fresh grapefruit juice

¼ cup champagne vinegar

1 tablespoon honey

2 teaspoons orange zest

Directions:

In a bowl combine the grapefruit juice, champagne vinegar, honey and orange zest. Whisk well until blended.

Slowly add in the canola oil, whisking constantly until the oil is blended in.

Serve immediately or store in the refrigerator in an airtight jar. Shake well before using.

Nutritional Information: Calories 128, Fat 14g, Protein 0g, Net Carbohydrates 2g

Blue Raspberry Dressing

Gluten Free, Vegan

Yields: 1 cup dressing, approximately 12 servings

Ingredients:

1 tablespoon extra virgin olive oil

½ cup balsamic vinegar

1 tablespoon sugar free raspberry preserves

¾ cup fresh blueberries

1 teaspoon lemon zest

Directions:

Place all of the ingredients in a blender or food processor. Blend until smooth.

Serve immediately or store in the refrigerator in an airtight jar until ready to serve.

Nutritional Information: Calories 21, Fat 1g, Protein 0g, Net Carbohydrates 3g

Papaya Mint Dressing

Gluten Free, Vegan

Yields: 1 cup dressing, approximately 8 servings

Ingredients:

1 tablespoon canola oil

¼ cup rice vinegar

2 tablespoons orange juice

1 papaya, cubed

1 tablespoon fresh mint, chopped

Directions:

Place the rice vinegar, orange juice and papaya in a blender. Blend until a puree forms.

Add in the canola oil and mint. Blend just until mixed.

If you prefer a thinner dressing, you can add more rice vinegar or orange juice to suit your liking.

Nutritional Information: Calories 31, Fat 2g, Protein 0g, Net Carbohydrates 4g

Orange Pomegranate Dressing

Gluten Free, Low Carb, Vegan

Yields:1½ cup dressing, approximately 12 servings

Ingredients:

½ cup extra virgin olive oil

3 tablespoons apple cider vinegar

¼ cup plus 1 tablespoon orange juice

1 tablespoon pomegranate juice

2 tablespoons orange zest

2 tablespoons pomegranate seeds

1 teaspoon salt

1 teaspoon coarse ground black pepper

Directions:

In a bowl combine the apple cider vinegar, pomegranate juice, orange juice, orange zest and pomegranate seeds.

Slowly stir in the olive oil, whisking until the dressing is well blended.

Season as desired with salt and black pepper.

Serve immediately or store in the refrigerator in an airtight jar. Shake well before using.

Nutritional Information: Calories 83, Fat 9g, Protein 0g, Net Carbohydrates 1g

Perfect Fruit Salad Dressing

Gluten Free

Yields: 1½ cup dressing, approximately 12 servings

Ingredients:

1 cup plain Greek yogurt

2 tablespoons coconut milk

¼ cup plus 1 tablespoon fresh lime juice

¼ cup honey

1 tablespoon fresh mint, chopped

2 teaspoons lime zest

Directions:

Place all of the ingredients in a blender and blend until smooth and creamy.

Serve immediately or store in the refrigerator in an airtight jar until ready to serve.

Nutritional Information: Calories 31, Fat 1g, Protein 2g, Net Carbohydrates 5g

Citrus Herb Dressing

Gluten Free, Low Carb, Vegan

Yields: 1 cup dressing, approximately 12 servings

Ingredients:

½ cup extra virgin olive oil

2 tablespoons champagne vinegar

2 tablespoons orange juice

2 tablespoons lime juice

2 tablespoons grapefruit juice

1 tablespoon lemon zest

1 tablespoon fresh mint, chopped

1 tablespoon fresh basil, chopped

½ teaspoon salt

Directions:

Combine the champagne vinegar, orange juice, lime juice, grapefruit juice, lemon zest, mint, basil and salt. Whisk together.

Slowly add in the olive oil, whisking constantly until well blended.

Serve immediately or store in the refrigerator in an airtight jar until ready to serve. Shake well before using.

Nutritional Information: Calories 83, Fat9g, Protein 0g, Net Carbohydrates 1g

Strawberry Basil Dressing

Gluten Free, Low Carb, Vegan

Yields: 1½ cup dressing, approximately 12 servings

Ingredients:

½ cup extra virgin olive oil

1 tablespoon balsamic vinegar

1 tablespoon lemon juice

1 cup strawberries, chopped

1 tablespoon fresh basil, chopped

½ teaspoon black pepper

Directions:

Place the balsamic vinegar, lemon, juice, strawberries, basil and black pepper in a blender. Blend until a puree forms.

Slowly add the olive oil, blending until completely mixed in.

Serve immediately or store in the refrigerator in an airtight jar until ready to serve.

Shake well before using.

Nutritional Information: Calories 85, Fat 9g, Protein 0g, Net Carbohydrates 1g

Tropical Heat Dressing

Gluten Free

Yields: 1½ cup dressing, approximately 16 servings

Ingredients:

½ cup canola oil

¼ cup rice vinegar

1 cup mango, chopped

2 teaspoons jalapeno pepper, diced

1 tablespoon honey

1 tablespoon lime juice

1 teaspoon lime zest

½ teaspoon salt

Directions:

Place the rice vinegar, mango, jalapeno pepper, honey and lime juice in a blender. Mix until a puree forms.

Slowly add in the canola oil, blending until fully mixed in.

Add in the lime zest and salt and then stir.

Serve immediately or store in the refrigerator in an airtight jar until ready to serve.

Nutritional Information: Calories 70, Fat 7g, Protein 0g, Net Carbohydrates 3g

Creamy Maple Dressing

Gluten Free

Yields: 1½ cup dressing, approximately 12 servings

Ingredients:

¼ cup plain Greek yogurt

¼ cup low fat mayonnaise

¼ cup apple cider vinegar

¼ cup plus 2 tablespoons pure maple syrup

½ teaspoon salt

1 teaspoon coarse ground black pepper

¼ cup pecans, chopped

Directions:

In a bowl combine the Greek yogurt, mayonnaise and apple cider vinegar. Whisk until well blended.

Whisk in the maple syrup until completely blended.

Season with salt and black pepper and stir in the chopped pecans.

Serve immediately or store in the refrigerator in an airtight jar until ready to serve.

Nutritional Information: Calories 24, Fat 1g, Protein 1g, Net Carbohydrates 4g

SPECIALTY BLENDER DRESSINGS (NUTRIBULLET, MAGIC BULLET, ETC.)

There are some incredible specialty blenders on the market today, each with features designed to make living a healthy lifestyle easier by encouraging you to explore new ways to enjoy fresh ingredients. One such way is an endless variety of fresh dressings for your salads. Most of these recipes are a simple one step process of tossing all of the ingredients in and blending, resulting in an almost instantaneous creation of perfect flavor and consistency.

Toasted Sesame Dressing

Low Carb, Vegan

Yields: 1 cup dressing, approximately 8 servings

Ingredients:

¼ cup lemon juice

¼ cup miso paste

¼ cup tahini

2 teaspoons sesame oil

1 tablespoon toasted sesame seeds

½ teaspoon salt

½ teaspoon black pepper

Directions:

Place all ingredients in the blender and blend until smooth.

Serve immediately or store in the refrigerator until ready to serve.

Nutritional Information: Calories 48, Fat 4g
Protein 1g, Net Carbohydrates 2g

Hot and Sour Asian Dressing

Low Carb

Yields: 1 ½ cup dressing, approximately 16 servings

Ingredients:

1 cup extra virgin olive oil

¼ cup rice vinegar

2 teaspoons sesame oil

2 cloves garlic

1 Serrano pepper, diced

¼ cup red bell pepper, diced

1 tablespoon miso

1 teaspoon honey

1 teaspoon salt

1 teaspoon black pepper

Directions:

Place the garlic, Serrano pepper, red bell pepper and miso to the blender. Blend until pulverized.

Next, add the olive oil, rice vinegar, sesame oil, honey, salt and black pepper. Blend until smooth.

Serve immediately or store in the refrigerator until ready to serve.

Nutritional Information: Calories 127, Fat 14g, Protein 0g, Net Carbohydrates 1g

Garden Herb Dressing

Low Carb, Gluten Free, Vegan

Yields: 1½ cup dressing, approximately 16 servings

Ingredients:

1 cup extra virgin olive oil

¼ cup lemon juice

¼ cup fresh basil, chopped

¼ cup fresh parsley, chopped

1 tablespoon fresh mint, chopped

1 tablespoon fresh oregano, chopped

1 teaspoon salt

1 teaspoon black pepper

Directions:

Place all of the ingredients in the blender and blend until smooth.

Serve immediately or store in the refrigerator until ready to serve.

Nutritional Information: Calories 120, Fat 13g, Protein 0g, Net Carbohydrates 0g

Creamy Cucumber Dill Dressing

Low Carb, Gluten Free

Yields: 1½ cup dressing, approximately 12 servings

Ingredients:

1 cup plain Greek yogurt

2 tablespoons lemon juice

2 tablespoons extra virgin olive oil

1 cup cucumber, sliced

1 tablespoon shallots, diced

¼ cup fresh dill

1 teaspoon salt

1 teaspoon black pepper

Directions:

Place the cucumber, shallots and dill in the blender. Blend until smooth.

Add in the Greek yogurt, lemon juice, olive oil, salt and black pepper. Blend until creamy.

Serve immediately or store in the refrigerator until ready to serve.

Nutritional Information: Calories 32, Fat 2g, Protein 2g, Net Carbohydrates 2g

Lemony Caesar Dressing

Low Carb, Gluten Free
Yields: 2 cups dressing, approximately 20
servings

Ingredients:
1 cup olive oil
¼ cup plus 1 tablespoon lemon juice
2 pasteurized eggs
1½ tablespoon shallots, diced
2 teaspoons lemon zest
¼ cup anchovies
½ cup fresh grated parmesan cheese
½ teaspoon salt
1 teaspoon coarse ground black pepper

Directions:
Add the shallots, lemon zest and anchovies to the
blender and blend to make a paste.

Add in the olive oil, lemon juice, eggs, parmesan
cheese, salt and coarse ground black pepper.
Blend until well mixed and lightly emulsified.

Nutritional Information: Calories 117, Fat 12g, Protein 2g, Net Carbohydrates 1g

Creamy Garlic Cilantro Dressing

Low Carb, Gluten Free

Yields: 1 ½ cup dressing, approximately 12 servings

Ingredients:

1 cup plain Greek yogurt

2 tablespoons extra virgin olive oil

¼ cup lime juice

3 cloves garlic

¼ cup fresh cilantro, chopped

¼ cup fresh parsley, chopped

½ teaspoon salt

1 teaspoon black pepper

Directions:

Place all of the ingredients in the blender and blend until smooth.

Serve immediately or store in the refrigerator until ready to serve.

Nutritional Information: Calories 32, Fat 26, Protein 2g, Net Carbohydrate 2g

Spinach Walnut Dressing

Low Carb

Yields: 1 ½ cup dressing, approximately 20 servings

Ingredients:

1 cup extra virgin olive oil

1 tablespoon walnut oil

¼ cup sherry vinegar

2 tablespoons shallots, diced

½ cup fresh spinach, torn

¼ cup walnuts, chopped

¼ cup goat cheese

Directions:

Place the shallots, spinach and walnuts in the blender. Blend until pulverized.

Add in the olive oil, walnut oil, sherry vinegar and goat cheese. Blend until well mixed and emulsified.

Serve immediately or store in the refrigerator until ready to serve.

Nutritional Information: Calories 110, Fat 12g, Protein 1g, Net Carbohydrates 1g

Peanut Soy Dressing

Low Carb

Yields: 2 cups dressing, approximately 20 servings

Ingredients:

1 cup canola oil

2 teaspoons sesame oil

½ cup rice vinegar

¼ cup creamy natural peanut butter

3 tablespoons soy sauce

1 tablespoon honey

¼ cup peanuts, chopped

½ teaspoon cayenne powder

½ teaspoon salt

1 teaspoon black pepper

Directions:

Place all of the ingredients in a blender and blend until smooth and creamy.

Serve immediately or store in the refrigerator until ready to serve.

Nutritional Information: Calories 122, Fat 12g, Protein 2g, Net Carbohydrates 1g

Honey Balsamic Vinaigrette

Low Carb, Gluten Free

Yields: 1 cup dressing, approximately 8 servings

Ingredients:

¾ cup extra virgin olive oil

¼ cup balsamic vinegar

2 cloves garlic

2 teaspoons honey

½ teaspoon salt

1 teaspoon coarse ground black pepper

Directions:

Place all of the ingredients in the blender and blend until emulsified.

Serve immediately or store in the refrigerator until ready to serve.

Nutritional Information: Calories 126, Fat 13g, Protein 0g, Net Carbohydrates 2g

Tangerine Scallion Dressing

Gluten Free

Yields: 1 ½ cup dressing, approximately 16 servings

Ingredients:

½ cup extra virgin olive oil

¼ cup champagne vinegar

2 tangerines, peeled

¼ cup scallions, chopped

2 cloves garlic

1 tablespoon honey

1 tablespoon fresh tarragon

½ teaspoon salt

1 teaspoon black pepper

Directions:

Add all of the ingredients to your blender. Blend until emulsified.

Serve immediately or store in the refrigerator until ready to serve.

Nutritional Information: Calories 70, Fat 7g, Protein 0g, Net Carbohydrates 3g

Avocado Cilantro Dressing

Low Carb, Gluten Free

Yields: 2 cups dressing, approximately 16 servings

Ingredients:

1 cup plain Greek yogurt

1 avocado, cubed

1 tablespoon lime juice

2 cloves garlic

¼ cup red bell pepper diced

¼ cup fresh cilantro, chopped

½ teaspoon salt

1 teaspoon pepper

Directions:

Place all of the ingredients in a blender and blend until smooth and creamy.

Serve immediately or store in the refrigerator until ready to use.

Nutritional Information: Calories 27, Fat 2g, Protein 2g, Net Carbohydrates 2g

Conclusion

Eating healthy takes a commitment to paying close attention to what you fuel your body with. The problem is that sometimes, even with attempts at creativity, healthy fueling can feel boring and redundant, especially when it comes to something like the basic salad. There is no reason that your salad, or what you dress it with needs to be anything other than delicious and inspirational to you along your path to good, lifelong health. No longer does a healthy salad mean one that is missing the pizzazz of a tangy and herb blessed dressing. It also doesn't mean that you are doomed to a life of choosing the bland "healthy" dressing from your grocer's shelves.

You can create dressings that support your healthy goals while leaving your taste buds excited and satisfied at once. We have come to a point where we view food as either fast or slow, with fast food being demonized while slow food is longed for but not achieved. True attainable healthy eating resides in the middle. These dressings are not the tasteless, processed fast food varieties, but they require so little of your time and effort that you will almost feel as though you are cheating at times. The right dressing is a little indulgence, one that satisfies cravings and your soul. Enjoy each and every one of them as you find new ways to explore and enjoy healthy eating.

Printed in Poland
by Amazon Fulfillment
Poland Sp. z o.o., Wrocław

50633936R00076